# A HUSBAND

# AND

# WIFE'S

# LOVE LETTER

# TO GOD

*How Pleasing God in Your Marriage Expresses Your Faith*

*and Love to God*

**JOHN AND RONETTE JOHNSON**

# Table of Contents

# Dedication

♥

We humbly dedicate our work in this book to our Heavenly Father, Jesus Christ, and the Holy Spirit. Your love, grace, sacrifice, strength, and kindness serve as our greatest examples. We are thankful for having been created for Your glory and for being set apart. Through divine wisdom and understanding, we can hear and receive Your messages—be it through the Bible, Your voice, our spiritual leaders, our marriage, or one another. You are the source of our hope and inspiration, for which we are truly grateful.

## We dedicate this book to each other.

To my beautiful wife, Ronette, your love and respect for me never waver despite all my quirks and flaws. The Jesus in you shines brightly through your actions, making it clear you are heaven-sent. Over the years, I have watched you embody the virtues of a Proverbs 31 woman and become a wonderful wife. You deserve more than the world can offer, so I promise to give you something better than the world ever could—I'll give you Jesus to the best of my ability. I am truly blessed to have you as my wife and eagerly anticipate what the future holds for our family.

"It had to be you, it had to be me, it had to be us, and it was all God."

*Your loving husband, John*

♥ ♥ ♥ ♥ ♥ ♥ ♥ ♥

## To my handsome husband, John,

I remember the first day we met as if it were yesterday. It felt as though our hearts hugged each other and have since never let go. You have truly become the husband beyond my dreams, and I honor God and thank Him for you every day. Our marriage is proof that kings and queens are meant for real-life love stories, not just fairy tales. Thank you for taking the time to say "Hey!" that first day we met. Thank you for seeing me with your heart and spirit, not just with your eyes. I have witnessed your growth from a young man into a godly, loving husband and a man of God. I am immensely excited about what I know God is doing through you. I am a grateful wife! I love you, honey!

*- Ronette*

We dedicate this book to our Divine Heart Couples community; you all are the real MVPs. You have become like an extended family to us. To those who have been following us for nearly ten years, thank you for staying with us throughout this journey.

If you're new to the Divine Heart Couples community, welcome! We are excited to have you join us on this beautiful journey.

We love you all and deeply appreciate your support and love. Please share this book and recommend it to someone who could benefit from the love poured into these pages.

# In Loving Memory

———————————— ♥ ————————————

Three extraordinary women whose impact on this world
and on us is truly unforgettable.


Apostle Julia D. Ford

Linda Johnson

Aunt Nidia

# Acknowledgments

❤

A special thank you to our Apostle, Owen E. Ford Jr., for inspiring us to take bold steps and to continue evolving. Your specific teachings on evolution and boldness have truly motivated us to complete this book. The example of perseverance you've set has paved the way, while the wisdom and knowledge you've imparted inspire us daily. Your hard work has not gone unnoticed, and we thank God for your obedience, guidance, and leadership.

> *"Sometimes you need to take a leap of faith, sometimes*
> *you need to take bold steps, and sometimes both."*
>
> *- Ronette Johnson (Quote inspired by Apostle O.)*

Thank you to our spiritual leaders and church family for your love and prayers. We appreciate and love you, TLC!

I also want to express my gratitude to my mother, Dearist, my sister, Desirra B., and my twin brother, Ronere. Each of them has played a significant role in my life, investing in me, whether they were aware of it or not. I am thankful for the love, support, and encouragement they have provided me.

Mom, your encouraging words for John and me have always been powerful and timely. They have not gone unnoticed. Thank you for being the amazing person you are.

Sister! My star, Desirra B., you're everything to me, and I thank you for our talks and texts (and yes, the talks from your son, De'Raye, too, lol). They always provide the balance I need and keep me laughing. I'm so glad you're my sister.

To my twin brother, Ronere, what can I say? You have been more than a brother; you've been a true friend to us. Thank you for always being there for us, thinking of me and my husband. When you heard about our book, you were the first to purchase it, even sending us triple the amount before the book was finished. We are extremely grateful for your support and generosity.

**Thank you!**

# Foreword

───────── ♥ ─────────

A beautiful, loving, and kind spirit; an encouraging, creative, and intelligent person who loves and serves God faithfully. A Proverbs 31 woman. A devoted sister, daughter, auntie, dog mom, wife, and friend. An author with many books yet to come. My greatest blessing. That's my wife, Ronette. Her name, meaning "Strong Counsel," suits her perfectly, reflecting her natural inclination to uplift others, whether she knows them or not.

It is time she shared one of her many gifts with the world. Ronette is not only an author; she possesses a remarkable writing talent. Additionally, she is the founder and CEO of our nonprofit organization, Divine Heart Couples, where she dedicates herself daily to our online ministry and community through emails, calls, texts, and social media.

"She hears from the Lord, and then she writes. God speaks to her, and she types." I've witnessed her up at 3 AM, perfectly content with her divine assignment. Over two years, God communicated with my wife in the middle of the night, guiding her to write this book. This journey reaffirms that God accomplishes His will through us in His own time and manner. One day, I awoke and said, "Baby, it's time to write the first book." This echoed a previous experience when guided by faith, we began packing for our first home long before finding it. God's message was clear: "Y'all are going to write the first book together." After sharing what she had already written, we embarked on writing this wonderful book as a team.

Ronette, the lead author and heart of this book, has poured her spirit, heart, time, and tears into it. I am proud of her and honored to be the co-author of her debut work.

Ronette exemplifies beauty, both inside and out. Many describe her as a gem, kind, caring, and patient as Job—a sentiment I wholeheartedly share.

Throughout the three years of writing together, this book—filled with encouragement, tips, and tools—has also enriched our marriage, reminding us that there is always space for growth. I am honored to present to you "*A Husband and Wife's Love Letter to God: How Pleasing God in Your Marriage Expresses Your Faith and Love to God.*"

I pray that God never ceases to speak to her and that she continues to hear His voice as she shares what God entrusts to her.

**John T. Johnson**

# Introduction

———————————— ♥ ————————————

*"Our marriage is our love letter to God."*

We have crafted this book as a beacon of hope and encouragement for those yearning for the joys of a happy, fulfilling marriage while deepening their relationship with God. "A Husband and Wife's Love Letter to God" provides tools and insights for navigating the journey toward a safe, healthy, and loving marriage. With God by your side, anything is possible. If you are romantic at heart, you'll cherish the exclusive insights into how we, the authors, met and the intimate details of our marriage woven throughout this book. God, the greatest Author, has written our love story. Thus, our marriage stands as an eternal tribute to God, serving as both an inspiration to all and a heartfelt thank you to Him. Our union is undoubtedly a divine connection and blessed union.

This book is penned by a husband-and-wife team aimed at wives, future wives, and husbands and future husbands. Its mission is to uplift and encourage those seeking divine love, whether you are struggling to believe, already hold belief, or simply need reminding that God remains faithful and sovereign over life and marriage, regardless of circumstances.

> *"The best part of your love story is that God is the Author. He knows who and what is best for you."*

Our devotion to God is reflected in our actions toward each other within our marriage. This encompasses our communication, compassion, forgiveness, sacrifice, grace, and respect. Our love also manifests through patience, kindness, and our responses to each other. We are humbled and grateful to be chosen by God to be a couple who, despite our flaws, are determined to forge a new legacy, breaking the generational cycle observed in our families, where our mothers were never married to our fathers.

We are not only setting goals for ourselves but also bearing witness to many wonderful and divine marriages in our surroundings and across the world today. What a blessing! We aspire to be godly examples for our children, providing them with a living testimony of a godly union they can see, hear, and read about.

We pray that the words God has inspired within us will enlighten, encourage, and inspire you and that the Holy Spirit will guide you further on this journey.

# Chapter 1

—————— ♥ ——————

## *Our Marriage Is a Love Letter, but not a Fairytale*

### *Imperfect Husband and Wife but A Perfect Marriage Union*

Let's be completely honest about it. Humans make mistakes; God does not. We are indeed a lovely match made in Heaven, yet we are far from perfect and make no pretense of being so. The beauty and uniqueness of our union, designed for love, growth, and serving the Lord together, is not our own doing. In the past, we've said things we didn't mean and would hesitate to say today—nothing outrageously crazy, but spoken in anger with the wrong tone. However, over the years, we've matured both individually and as a godly couple.

In recent times, especially during the COVID years, the internet and social platforms have been rife with stories of breakups. We've heard all sorts of strange and unsettling news about relationships. Yet, let's take a moment to celebrate the amazing marriages God has brought together!

As you read this book, we hope you can think of at least one godly marriage. They may not be perfect, but they live for and love Jesus. Perhaps you know a couple who has overcome significant challenges—this is a testament to God's grace in their lives. And if you're married, may your own love story inspire you the most, as it should.

To our single brothers and sisters, we pray that your future marriage will be your most cherished testimony and an inspiring love story for others.

While we cannot offer specific advice for personal issues—since each relationship is unique—we emphasize the importance of treating one another with respect, kindness, and care. Be authentic yet gentle. Though every marriage is different, we all share the same God and His unchanging word. What the Bible says about marriage stands as our ultimate guide and instruction. God's word is eternal and unchanging. By standing on His word, God will support and guide you through life's challenges.

*Isaiah 40:7-8 ESV tells us that while the physical world may fade, God's word endures forever.*

We may not all function in the same way, but we should all live under the guidance of the same God. Our imperfections are not excuses for not giving our best every day—even if your best is simply making it through the day.

Remember, nobody is perfect, including your spouse. I am grateful for my understanding husband, just as I strive to be an understanding wife.

It wasn't always this way for us, so we pray our story encourages you. Remember, you are graced by the Lord for this journey. You've got this!

Seeking therapy and counseling is beneficial, but always turn to the Mighty Counselor, the Prince of Peace in Heaven, the first, last, and always. Prayer, fasting, and daily Bible study are vital ways to connect with God. Ask Him to bring divine connections into your life—people who support and uplift you. God will always provide support and a plan.

> *"With God, there's a happily ever after, not a happy ending."*

Yes, there will be unhappy moments and obstacles, but a joyful and content life is possible regardless of the challenges. God's everlasting nature means that our joy, rooted in Him, should never end. The resurrection of Jesus is a powerful reminder that what may seem like the end is just the beginning. Let us learn from our shortcomings, forgive quickly, and trust in God's perfection. We are created to please Him, and despite our failings, we must never forget His grace and strive to make Him proud.

## Colossians 3:13 NLT

*Make allowance for each other's faults, and forgive anyone who offends you. Remember, the Lord forgave you, so you must forgive others*

─────────────────── ♥ ───────────────────

*"Lord, bless me with a marriage that's out of this world. A marriage of your word, not of this world."*

*- Ronette J.*

─────────────────── ♥ ───────────────────

# Chapter 2

———————— ♥ ————————

## Identity, Partnership, and Friendship

*"Someone will see your worth because they kept their eyes on God."*
*- Ronette Johnson*

### Your Identity in Christ Jesus as Individuals and as a Couple

What do people perceive when they see you individually and as a couple? I absolutely adore the compliment, "Y'all look good together!" Indeed, you may be a visually appealing couple, but remember, as a godly pair, your actions and demeanor should mirror God's values—becoming a "God-looking couple." "When my partner and I both reflect God's image, that's when 'we look good together.'"

*"He must increase, but I must decrease." John 3:30 ESV*

Your relationship with God should take precedence, both before and after marriage. It's the compass that guides

9

you through life's fluctuations and provides strength in adversity. Cultivating your spiritual life is crucial for a fulfilling marriage. Through your relationship with Jesus, you'll discover the joy of solitude, learning that being alone doesn't mean loneliness. God's presence is a constant, even in moments of solitude.

Understanding your identity in Christ is vital. A relationship, marriage, and spouse are blessings from God, but they do not define you. Sis, your new or future last name signifies your connection with your spouse and marriage, but your primary identity remains as a child of God. Similarly, Bro, you are first and foremost a child of God, even before becoming a husband.

Realizing Jesus's unconditional love for you, despite flaws and errors, should inspire forgiveness and grace towards yourself, your spouse, and others. As you both grow to resemble God more closely, your spouse will be drawn to your divine spirit.

**Partnership and Friendship**

My spouse is unequivocally my best friend. A robust friendship is essential for a thriving, joyous, and enduring marriage. Your spouse should be your confidante through life's challenges, be it work-related issues, family dilemmas, or personal struggles. Thus, it's crucial to foster this friendship and maintain a strong connection.

Men, it's perfectly acceptable to be vulnerable with her. Single men, aim to build a friendship first, then pursue marriage. Friendship breeds trust. When faced with marital challenges, remembering your spouse as your best friend will remind you of your deep connection. "If you don't want my spouse to know your secrets, don't tell me," I often say. We are unified in our discretion.

Friendship within marriage encourages openness. Our family, friends, and even strangers have witnessed our inseparable bond since our relationship began. Our shared interests in sports, food, adventure, and serving the Lord have only strengthened our bond over eight years of marriage.

Early in our relationship, we learned the importance of teamwork, with "Coach Christ" guiding us. Remember, you and your partner are not just teammates but helpmates, designed to support each other in unique ways.

*"And the Lord God said, It is not good that the man should be alone; I will make him a help meet for him." Genesis 2:18 KJV*

**To our single brothers and sisters**, envision a future in a secure marriage that will last because God was always first.

**To all singles and married couples**, we pray this message encourages you to prioritize God. He will reveal your true identity, both individually and as a couple.

---❤---

*"Bro and Sis, you are God's before you are your spouse's, and that's what will draw your godly spouse closer to you."*

*- Ronette J.*

---❤---

# Chapter 3

♥

## A Kingdom Mindset: Pleasing God Before Your Pleasures

*"If you go to God first, you won't need a last resort." - Ronette Johnson*

When I consider what a Kingdom mindset entails, it revolves around prioritizing and honoring "the KING," God, above all—striving to please Him first and foremost. It's about dedicating every aspect of our lives to the glory of God.

In our Divine Heart Couples online ministry/community, our focus on God is deliberate. Indeed, almost every post is intertwined with God's presence because He is central to our existence. Our deepest desire is to honor God through our hearts, words, lives, and actions, hoping that our marriage reflects His divine approval.

*Matthew 6:33 KJV*

*"But seek ye first the kingdom of God, and his righteousness; and all these things shall be added unto you."*

*1 Corinthians 10:31 KJV*

*"Whether therefore ye eat, or drink, or whatsoever ye do, do all to the glory of God."*

> *"We desire for God to see His reflection in the unseen aspects of our marriage."*

Acknowledging our imperfections, we aim to present our best selves, reliant on God's grace and mercy to cover our shortcomings.

Hebrews 11:6 states, "But without faith, it is impossible to please Him: for he that cometh to God must believe that He is, and that He is a rewarder of them that diligently seek Him."

Let's delve into this concept! Firstly, pleasing God must be a heartfelt desire. Secondly, this desire necessitates faith. Thirdly, entering marriage—or any endeavor—with the intention of glorifying God ensures that everything else will align according to His will.

Consider this: actions undertaken in the name of Jesus Christ, without of faith, fall short of God's expectations.

Belief is essential. Moreover, the Bible teaches that faith without works is dead. It's crucial to animate our faith with actions, even if it begins with deepening our understanding of the Word of God. Whether single or married, there is always an opportunity to grow as a servant of God.

———————— ♥ ————————

*"When you honor God with your marriage, God will honor your marriage."*

*- John Johnson*

———————— ♥ ————————

*"Plug in and stay connected to God, your power source, resource, and outlet."*

*- Ronette J.*

———————— ♥ ————————

# Chapter 4

♥

## Date Someone with Integrity and Intentions to Marry

*"A lot of people will be attracted to you in many ways, but it's different when God sends your spouse to see what others cannot see."*
*- John and Ronette*

*Dear Singles,*

Firstly, remember that not just anyone deserves the chance to date you. Seek a partner who demonstrates their love for God through their actions. Before even considering a date, pray about your heart posture and theirs. Ask God to reveal any areas in you or them that may need attention before pursuing a relationship. Even before connecting over a phone call, seek guidance from the Holy Spirit. Request that God shows you whether this potential connection is divinely intended. Observe their life closely—though not to the point of stalking, of course. Review their social media, ask meaningful questions, and then pray for God to unveil their true character. If their actions don't align with their words, take a moment to consult with God. It's wise to have a trusted friend or someone with discernment to take a look as well. While extending grace and patience is okay, consider how long they truly need to be genuine if they are as they claim.

Verify their single status, their prayer life, and whether they initiate prayer with you without prompting. Assess their character, their faith, and their intentions. These questions are crucial in discerning their suitability as a partner. They might not be perfect, but their connection should be with the One who is perfect. This connection provides a solid foundation built on Jesus, fostering growth both as individuals and together. Remember, it's "Better safe now than sad and broken later."

**Bro,** a woman of God will discern if you embody more of God's qualities than worldly ones. The virtues of a Proverbs 31 woman will not allow her to settle for less. Your godliness cannot be feigned; if she is close to God, she will understand what qualities a godly husband should possess.

**Sis,** a man of God will recognize a godly spirit in his future wife. He'll know whether you have a genuine relationship with the Lord. However, not every good man you meet is destined to be your husband. A man of God recognizes that a woman of God will exhibit qualities of a Proverbs 31 wife even before marriage, as she is already in a committed relationship with God first and foremost. Her love for God is eternal, knowing He will never leave her nor forsake her.

*When she speaks, her words are wise, and she gives instructions with kindness. She carefully watches everything in her household and suffers nothing from laziness.* **Proverbs 31:26-27 NLT**

*"He was chasing after God and ran into his wife along the way."*

*- John Johnson*

# Chapter 5

———————— ♥ ————————

## *Planted Together to Bring Forth Fruit*

*"A couple can grow together when it's God who planted them together."*

**- Ronette Johnson**

Make sure God said, "Yes, that's your spouse." because you can only handle what is meant for you.

*Singles,* try not to rush what God wants to reserve. Be sure you are ready. Sometimes, it's just not time yet and sometimes, we as humans find ourselves in relationships or situations that are draining, miserable, or too much to handle. If you feel any of that, that is God revealing your worth to you and letting you know something is off. Those are signs you should never ignore. Pray to God for the strength and wisdom to remove yourself from a place where your worth is unwelcomed or unseen. You should also seek counseling, help from a trustworthy, reliable source, or ask a good friend with discernment to help point you in the right direction.

**They may not be your spouse if…**

- If the relationship is too much for you and it's weighing you down mentally, spiritually, physically, emotionally, financially, etc.

- If you don't feel a little sunlight when you're with them. Can they be a ray of sunshine on a cloudy day?

- If the soil is dry and not soft. They're hard to deal with and never positive. *No one is perfect, but when you address situations, see if they care.*

- If there is a lack of communication or none at all. Do they want to grow and communicate? Or do they feel that it's too hard to try?

- If they are stagnant. Are they being watered and nourished? They should desire to be planted in God, hopefully planted at a church. If not, check to see what their future plans are about being planted at a bible teaching church—on good ground. Have they started watching an online or TV church service? There are many options with the technology we have in the world today.

You can also relate the above info to yourself. Are you really ready to be married and planted together *forever?* Are you ready to be fruitful and multiply together with one person in many ways? Finding a divine heart that loves you back is exciting! If you both are being watered, you can pour good things back into each other.

**A few things that indicate that a person/relationship is planted in God.**

- Good ground, good soil. (They are planted and serve at a Bible-based teaching church/online member). *There are some exceptions, such as maybe you don't have a church home yet. Maybe y'all can find one together.*

- Nourishment (They have a prayer and Bible study life even outside of the church building.)

- Blooming (individually and together in many areas).

- Growth (You see changes for better. The small steps are just as important as the big leaps of Faith.)

- They are confident in who God created them to be. (Sometimes this can take time and they should be willing to accept help in that area.)

- A sprouting marriage. (Even though marriages will face challenges sometimes, they can grow in grace when they are in God's will.)

God wants you to live out your marriage purpose with your partner, but even if you are not there yet, today you can take some destiny steps toward becoming a better person and a good and faithful servant of God.

---- ♥ ----

*"Seeing your spouse become the person God created them to be. That's Attractive."*

*- Ronette Johnson*

---- ♥ ----

*"A man of God is great by himself, but his godly wife comes to help fulfill God's promise."*

*- Ronette J.*

---- ♥ ----

# Chapter 6

♥

## Divine Timing and Patiently Waiting

*"God hid them to heal them. Then God sent him to find her, all in His divine timing."*

**- John and Ronette**

*"Love is patient and kind."* Some people will not understand why you believe God and His timing because they did not give you your belief. Your faith came from God, your source.

*"You have to see it as already done in the spirit first."*

*- Dearist Elaine Williams*

Some people just don't believe. You can't expect people to have the same expectations you have when it isn't for them. It's for you.

### 1 Corinthians 13:4-7 NLT

*[4] Love is patient and kind. Love is not jealous or boastful or proud [5] or rude. It does not demand its own way. It is not irritable, and it keeps no record of being wronged. [6] It does not rejoice about injustice but rejoices whenever the truth wins out. [7] Love never gives up, never loses faith, is always hopeful, and endures through every circumstance.*

*"The best part of your love story is that God is the Author. He knows who, when, and what is best for you."*

*- Ronette Johnson*

―――――――――― ♥ ――――――――――

*"Ladies,*

*It does not take a man long to know if he sees favor, forever, and a future with you."*

*- John and Ronette*

―――――――――― ♥ ――――――――――

# Chapter 7

♥

## Intentions and Preparation for Marriage

*Any woman can make a beautiful bride. A good*
*wife is what a husband needs."*

### - Ronette Johnson

Are you ready to become one? Did you know that two people in a marriage can be together for a long time but still not be in oneness?

If you're single, ask yourself this question.

*Why do I want to get married?*

If you're married, ask yourself this question.

*Why did I want to get married?*

**The importance of having pure and good intentions.**

Firstly, you should desire a marriage that will bring glory and honor to God, and you should want to get married because you want to please God first. Not because you just want to have sex, you love the idea of marriage, or just because you see others getting married. Yes, a godly marriage includes many benefits, but pleasing God should be a priority.

> *"Marriage is not a fairytale, it's real life."*

*"I want our marriage to be an example of what God said in the scriptures about what love and marriage should be."*

*- Ronette Johnson*

**Are you really prepared?**

I've heard people say, "You can never be prepared for anything, including marriage." From experience and from what I've been told, the truth is you can be a little prepared for something but not completely ready. That makes a lot of sense.

Although when you get married, you really don't know all the details and things you'll come up against, know that God knows every detail of your life and He is already protecting you from seen and unseen dangers. It's important to marry a person who loves and fears the Lord. You need someone who you can speak to mountains with. You need someone who's anointed like you are.

*"Matching clothes and pjs are cute, but can you match my anointing too?"*

*- Ronette J.*

Pleasing God should be the first goal. Don't worry, God will make sure you enjoy your marriage, too! Serving the Lord is worth it.

———————— ♥ ————————

*"I pray that one day, you will dance with your spouse like God is the only one watching, with or without music, but dancing to the beat of God's heart."*

*- Ronette J.*

———————— ♥ ————————

# Chapter 8

♥

## Prayer Partners For Life

*"When the person you prayed for becomes the person you pray with."*

- @divineheartcouples "John and Ronette"

We cannot give y'all the exact prayers that we prayed. Lol, but you should be clear with God on what your heart's desires are. If your desires don't align with God's will as you get closer to God, pray daily, and read the Bible, your prayers and desires may just shift to what God's will is for you. Amen! God Knows what's best for us and will change our approach and appetite for love so it will align with His will for us. All along while you're praying every day, God is protecting you, the promise, your marriage, and His legacy.

I remember those times when I was younger and I started praying for my husband. I just knew that my husband had to be a man who loves the Lord. Funny thing is I was not sure about all that I needed or wanted lol, but God knew.

*John is what I never knew I needed and what I've never seen in anyone else. He's my earth angel.*

*- Ronette*

*I remember being young and praying for a wife. I have always desired to marry a woman of God that is beautiful inside and out. God did the rest and gave me more than I could ever dream of. I asked God to show me a piece of Heaven, and He blessed me with my beautiful wife.*

*- John*

## Praying Together

What we do that works for us. We choose a time and place every day that works for us and we pray not only for ourselves, but for others, and even strangers. We also have weekly Bible Study at home. But we're both so random! We switch it up sometimes, and a praise and worship session can break out at any time. Even a praise dance from time to time, lol.

So, for prayer, choose a time that works for both of you. A time where you won't have to rush the prayer, not saying it has to be super long either. Whatever and however God leads you is perfectly up to God and y'all. But it's best if you do not rush any time you spend with God or your partner, so schedule wisely!

Praying together can start in your dating season. Even when you're not physically in the same place, you can pray over the phone, facetime, video, etc. If you cannot talk on the phone, instead of just a "Good morning text," send "A morning prayer." Some phones have voice text messages, and that's a great way to send a prayer as well.

*Dear Singles,* if you are waiting and not currently dating, never stop including your future spouse in your prayers.

— ♥ —

*"He prayed for her, she prayed for him, God answered them both in His divine timing."*

*- @divineheartcouples "John and Ronette"*

— ♥ —

---- ♥ ----

*"When a couple prays together, their voices in harmony are like good music to God's ears."*

*- Ronette J.*

---- ♥ ----

# Chapter 9

♥

## A Divine Connection

*"When you meet someone and the Jesus in them recognizes the Jesus in you."*

*"Hallelujah!"*

*- Ronette Johnson*

When we first met, our very first conversation was about God and then we also talked about God every day in our conversations. But it wasn't until we started having deep and honest conversations with God together that we began to fully understand that our relationship and connection was divine. We were meant to meet and join in holy matrimony for God's glory.

*Dear singles,* if you're on the dating scene and looking for a meaningful relationship, it's essential to be upfront about your faith. Don't hesitate to let your potential partner know that your love for Jesus Christ is an integral part of your life. This way, you'll ensure that you're building a relationship with someone who shares your values and beliefs. Remember, honesty is key when it comes to finding true love.

Do you know how some toys or items say "batteries included" on the packaging? Let the person interested in dating you know that you and your future marriage come with "Jesus already included." An all-in-one package deal. "You, your spouse, the Father, the Son, and the Holy Spirit."

So, we met about two weeks or so after I finished college. I was absolutely not looking for a man or anything, I was only eager and excited to be starting a new job in the IT field. Plus, I was already halfway out of a situationship, and I just did not care to be bothered. I remember the first time I looked up at that young man saying, "Get off my computer." I was working on an IT project in the shipping area and honestly, I thought, "Oh God, what does this guy want?" I also thought he was very handsome. Easy on the eyes still to this day. Now, he is my husband!

We talked a whole lot, mostly about God. We started telling our testimonies to each other until someone came looking for me. John almost got me in trouble my 2nd week working with the company, lol, and the rest is our legacy.

We have not been perfect and never will be, but one thing for sure is we both love the Lord with our whole hearts. We just want to continue to bring glory to His name through our lives and our marriage. When we met, it was like Jesus was connecting with Himself through us. Talk about a divine connection! God did his thing with this union! A match truly made in Heaven, not only because of the good things but also all the things we are not. We have grown through a lot and we are still growing and accomplishing goals.

Honestly, In the beginning, it did feel like what some would call "a fairytale", but God quickly shut that down and reminded us daily that this is real life. It was better than a fairytale! It still is. "Our Marriage is our happily ever after and a beautiful love letter to God."

*"I get to see my soul mate not be perfect but still view him in a different light. The light of Christ." - Ronette*

*"I get to see the glow of God show through my wife, and even though she is not perfect, she's perfect for me."*
*- John*

Woman of God/Man of God, that's when you know it's real.

God does not play games. It literally will be God connecting with Himself through y'all connection. That's a different kind of connection. A divine connection.

*Ladies*, you're not just looking for a beard and good looks.

*You're not looking to see Santa; you're looking for the gift of Jesus Christ!*

## Love Quotes

♥

*"I love it when you kiss me because it always feels like destiny is planted every time your lips touch me."* - *Your wife, Ronette*

*"This isn't just love, this isn't just a feeling, this is divine destiny."*

*- Your husband, John*

*"It's different when it's not forced and it's God's timing."*

*- Ronette J.*

# Chapter 10

♥ ———

## Privacy and Security, Leave and Cleave.

*"Nothing should come between a marriage but God. And that's to keep them together."*

*- John Johnson*

**Being present in a private relationship**

Humbly, I think we are doing great in this area. There should be a level of privacy and security for your marriage. This goes for your family and friends, and strangers too.

We know most people in your lives mean well, but it is not their place to tell you how to handle situations in your life or marriage. There's nothing wrong with receiving "some" godly advice from those who have experience in a certain area, but you should have a level of respect and privacy for your spouse and marriage. Be certain your spouse agrees with whom you share info with. That way, there are no surprises.

Marriage coaching and counseling works. You should look for coaches/counselors with integrity and whom you can trust. Ask God to send divine connections and give you discernment to know and see who they truly are.

As for us, John and Ronette, people only know what we tell them. "People only know what we show them. Everything else they just assume." We like it like that.

> *"Privacy is one of our favorite places to be."*

Status: offline

Mood: offline

**Leave and Cleave**

Are you ready to become ONE with your spouse? Becoming one in your marriage is a necessity.

> *"You cannot become one if you don't leave and cleave."*

- Leave means to go away from.
- Cleave means to stick fast to.

Regardless of what people may think or say about you and your spouse, y'all have to leave the old ways of thinking behind and welcome the new way that honors God through your marriage.

You have to know that your spouse is part of your new family and they come first, after God.

## Genesis 2:24 NKJV

*Therefore, a man shall leave his father and mother and be joined to his wife, and they shall become one flesh.*

*"If God said it and wrote it, then it's possible. Yes, it's possible for two people to become one in a marriage."*

*- Ronette J.*

# Chapter 11

♥

## No Comparison and No Competition

Your marriage is one of one. Never forget that.

*A wise pastor once preached a message (that had nothing to do with marriage) when I was younger, and it has stayed with me until this day. "Your Greatness is in your Difference."*

*- Pastor Gilbert A. Snowden*

I know it's hard for some people not to compare, especially with the glitz and glamorous posts we see on social media today. But there's absolutely no marriage like your marriage. You have no competition. Marriage is not a game, and it's not a fairytale. It is real life, and real life and marriage can be amazing with the right person.

# Chapter 12

❤

## *Husbands, Lead with Love and Wives Follow with Respect*

**Husbands, Lead with Love**

Unfortunately, some men aren't taught to lead or how to lead correctly, so they have to learn. No big deal to a big God. "Let's all relax and breathe here."

Every man does not grow up having a good example of what a godly husband looks like. It's okay; this is where God steps in and shows you how He's going to get the glory out of this, too.

***Man of God,*** pray for God to send you divine connections only. Men of wisdom and integrity who can teach you how to submit to God and lead your wife/future wife. Pray for your wife to submit to God first and for y'all to submit unto one another. Yes, I used that word. We all have to accept the whole Bible.

*Woman of God,* you want the loving and caring husband and He wants the respect, respect, the respect, and the sex. Okay, well, he needs love and grace, too. But allow him to be the godly husband that God created him to be. Trust him as He follows Christ.

*Ladies,*

When you trust your "godly" husband to lead, you're trusting God to lead you both.

*Husbands and future husbands*, stay in prayer about your wife's mind, body, heart, and spirit. She has so much to take on each day. She works and takes care of the home and children, you, the dog and cat, bird, and the frog, too. In addition to that, she may even run a business or help out in the community. Pray that she does not let the pressures of society's standards pressure her.

**Wives Follow with Respect as He Follows Christ.**

*Wives and future wives,* stay in prayer for your husband. Pray for his mindset. Pray for the things he watches and what he gives his attention and energy to. Pray that he will lead a life that is pleasing to God and God's grace will cover him when he falls short. Yes, he will fall short and so will you. Still pray about it, though. Pray for God to protect and guide your husband. Pray that he will be faithful and trust God to lead the way so much that he will begin to lead easily.

I can admit I had issues submitting and allowing my husband to lead at the beginning of our marriage. Not anymore, because I see him truly following the Lord to the best of his ability, and I have put my full trust in God, our true leader.

Back in 2017, two years after we were married, a beautiful and wise woman of God, the late Apostle Julia D. Ford prophesied over our marriage and one of the things she confirmed was that it was okay to let my husband lead. She said, "You've gotten you both this far; he has got it from here now. Allow him to lead." Before that day, Apostle J had never met us and neither of us had spoken a single word to her or anyone she knows. Look at God!

---❤---

*"Bro,*

*Leading your wife is easier when God is your leader.*
*You have a reliable source to point you in the right*
*direction, and she can trust you to lead when she*
*knows God is leading the way."*

*- John Johnson*

---❤---

# Chapter 13

♥

## *Love, Communication, Space and Grace*

### *Your Spouse Needs Their Alone Time and You Need Your Alone Time*

This applies before and after you get married. You should always make time for yourself. Spend time with yourself and get to know you, and you'll see that there are some things about you that you need to allow grace in, areas you need to grow in, and areas you need to heal in. As you grow, you will learn to live and love yourself with your flaws and all.

This takes me back to the very first chapter of this book, where it mentions that none of us are perfect. If you are struggling with self-love or anything else, it's okay to seek help from a reliable and trustworthy source. Seek God, and find a therapist, preferably one who is a believer of Jesus Christ. Also, know that reading the Bible is a great source for understanding and learning to love yourself. You can search the internet for "Bible scriptures about loving yourself and comfort."

Okay, so let's talk about your amazing spouse/future spouse! Your spouse will need their time alone. In order to maintain a healthy and happy relationship with your spouse, it is crucial to understand and respect each other's need for alone time. Taking time for yourself to relax and recharge is just as important as spending time together. It's imperative to communicate openly and honestly with your partner about your need for alone time and encourage them to do the same. By doing so, you can avoid unnecessary conflicts and build a stronger, more fulfilling relationship. Remember, a little alone time can go a long way!

In their life and marriage, they need the grace to grow and the forever space to allow themselves to just be who they are all the time. "It's okay." They are who they are and if you love them and pray for them every day, right where they are, God will do the changing, shaping, and the molding.

Although people try to do this a lot, it is not a human's job to change other humans; God does that. People can change after surrendering their hearts to the Lord and submitting their ways to Him. Pray for them to submit to God.

Space is a must in any relationship. Even family and friendships need boundaries. And last but not least, you both will constantly need alone time to be with God. My best time alone is when it's with my first love, my Heavenly Father. Where He does what my family, friends, spouse, dog, or success will never be able to do.

*"I love when the Creator makes me over and shapes and molds me to be more like Him."*

*- Ronette J.*

*A loving partner creates space for their significant other to grow, as love requires patience.*

---❤---

*"A God-sent will take the time to learn how God designed you to be loved. Your standards are not too high. God created you to be loved at a high level."*

*- Ronette J.*

---❤---

# Chapter 14

♥

## A Love Letter

***If our marriage could actually speak words to God, here's an example of the love letter so far.***

Dear **Abba Father**,

You are everything to us. Our greatest notification in the morning when we wake up, the voice we can't wait to hear throughout the day and at night before bed.

You are our peace. Your love is the greatest love we've ever felt, experienced, and known. Your wisdom is like an ever-flowing river that keeps on giving. Only you could ever take credit for this beautiful union, and we will give you praise and glory for it daily. We are a match made in Heaven for real. You have carefully crafted us and perfectly matched two imperfect people. Thank you for your continued grace, mercy, and forgiveness as we continue to learn about love, life, and marriage every day. We adore you.

Dear **Jesus,**

You blow our minds with what you have done for us. Your sacrifice is unmatched. You are the center of our love and joy, our greatest example of being selfless, loving, and compassionate. You are beauty, grace, and strength. You're the reason we can forgive quickly, give grace, and love each other better. You're our anchor. Thank you for healing us from life's past hurts. By your stripes, we are truly healed.

Dear **Holy Spirit**,

You have led and guided us in love thus far and we trust you as we continue this journey. You are our helper. You are our teacher. You give us discernment and we feel your presence everywhere we go. You're always with us. This is a forever love.

God, we love because you first loved us and this marriage belongs to you. We love you!

With love from our whole hearts,

John and Ronette

———————— ♥ ————————

*"Regardless of your past, God wants you to know that you're more than enough for the future He has planned for you."*

*- John Johnson*

———————— ♥ ————————

# Epilogue

♥

Whether you are a hopeless romantic, hopeful and in love, or embarking on a new chapter, adventure, or journey in your life, we pray that God will meet you right where you are and give you hope and faith that nothing or no one on this earth or in hell can steal. We pray that you would get to know Jesus Christ for yourself and let Him show you how much He loves you. We pray that you would cast all your cares on the Lord for He cares for you. Know that the Bible says in 1 Peter 5:7 to Give all your worries and cares to God, for he cares about you.

To those who may be struggling, God calls you worthy. God cares about you. He cares about your pain and He wants to heal you. We pray for a healed version of you to come forth in every area of your life, your mind, heart, spirit, soul, and body in the mighty name of Jesus, we pray, Amen.

Please pray and ask God to give you the strength, courage, faith, and hope you need through His son Jesus Christ. I pray that God will give you a drive in your heart and spirit that no doubter could ever sway. Not even your own thoughts. You must guard your heart from the enemy and people who want to make you doubt God. You have those desires in your heart for a reason. God wants to fulfill them. We can attest that joy will make its way to you, and it'll be there to stay regardless of your circumstances.

Our Marriage is our love letter to God. A letter that we will add more to every day as we will never stop growing and learning about ourselves, God, life, family, love, and marriage. It's a love letter with no ending. "It's not a fairytale with a happy ending, but a beautiful marriage and love story with plenty of new beginnings."

We are thankful for a fresh and new wind every day and for daily renewal. "His mercies are new every morning!"

You've made it this far in this book; we pray that you have read something that will prompt change and growth in many areas and that something you read was encouraging and heartwarming. We desire to continue to be a light in this world that can be dark at times, and we pray we can help bring hope to every person who reads this book.

# Bonus Material!

♥

We will leave you with a few of our favorite Bible scriptures.

### Proverbs 4:23 NLT

*Guard your heart above all else, for it determines the course of your life.*

### Proverbs 18:22 NKJV

*He who finds a wife finds a good thing, and obtains favor from the Lord.*

### Ephesians 5:25 NLT

*For husbands, this means love your wives, just as Christ loved the church. He gave up his life for her.*

### Ephesians 5:28-33 NLT

*28 In the same way, husbands, ought to love their wives as they love their own bodies. For a man who loves his wife actually shows love for himself. 29 No one hates his own body but feeds and cares for it, just as Christ cares for the church. 30 And we are members of his body.*

*31 As the Scriptures say, "A man leaves his father and mother and is joined to his wife, and the two are united into one." 32 This is a great mystery, but it is an illustration of the way Christ and the church are one. 33 So again I say, each man must love his wife as he loves himself, and the wife must respect her husband.*

### Psalm 37:4 NLT

*Take delight in the Lord, and he will give you your heart's desires.*

# About the Authors

John and Ronette are a husband-and-wife team who have been happily married since 2015. They are active in their church as they are humble, faithful followers of Jesus Christ. Internationally known for their social media ministry/community turned nonprofit organization @ DivineHeartCouples, established in 2015 with now over 120,000 Instagram followers across the world.

Ronette has known about her unique gift of writing for many years and has finally published the first of many books to come. She has always been a hopeful romantic and has a love for reading books about love and marriage, including the Bible. She has a heart after God and is passionate about uplifting singles, husbands and wives, and anyone she comes across. Born and raised in Chester, PA, USA. Founder and CEO of Divine Heart Couples. Ronette is an intelligent, dedicated IT professional known for her kindness, creativity, wit, grit, and determination. Even though she has a twin, she is truly one of one.

John was raised in Sharon Hill, PA and has always known he was different as a small child. As he grew older, he knew he wanted to inspire people and help lead souls to Jesus. He is truly a man after God's own heart. John is a loving husband, the co-founder of Divine Heart Couples and has a heart to encourage singles and married couples alongside his wife, Ronette. He's passionate about God and the Bible, giving, evangelism, and marriage God's way.

Join them and stay connected on Instagram and Facebook @divineheartcouples and learn more about them and their ministry at their website: www.divineheartcouples.com

www.ingramcontent.com/pod-product-compliance
Lightning Source LLC
LaVergne TN
LVHW022324080426
835508LV00041B/2649

9 780099 152029 9